How Things Move

by Catherine Quirin

Understanding Movement

Suppose a boy is doing homework with his friend. His younger sister asks if she can play. He tells her he needs to study and she must sit still. His sister jumps and dances. Then she moves across the room to do a headstand!

The sister changes **position** when she moves from one spot to another. She is in **motion** when she changes position.

Her position changes compared to her brother's. First she is in front of him. Then she is behind him. Both of these positions can be called a **relative position** because it changes when compared to her brother's position.

How fast are these cars moving? Speed is a measurement of how fast or slow something changes position. The cars on the highway are moving forward very quickly. Other things, such as tortoises, move slowly.

Earth moves at a constant speed.

Objects often change speeds, such as from fast to slow. Other times, objects move at the same speed. When an object moves at the same speed, it moves at a constant speed. Earth is something that moves at a constant speed.

How fast or slow an object moves is not the only thing that can change. An object can also change direction. It can move forward, backward, sideways, or even in a circle. Sometimes an object can move quickly going forward, but must slow down to move backward or sideways. That object would move at a variable speed. Its speed changes as it moves in different directions.

Force

You make things move every day. You probably pull open a drawer to get some socks each morning. Then you push the drawer closed. Any push or pull is called **force.** The position of the drawer changed because you used force.

Most of the forces that you use are contact forces. This means that you touch, or make contact with, the object you wish to move. How much an object moves depends on how much force you use. The greater the force placed on an object, the more the object will move.

**Could you
move a wall?**

Sometimes you can use a lot of force to try
to move an object, but it does not move much
or at all. If you push against a wall, would you
be able to move it? Probably not, because the
amount of force you use is not enough to move
an object with as much mass as a wall. The greater
the mass of an object, the greater the force needed
to move it.

You can slide a desk across a classroom that has a smooth tile floor. Could you move the desk as easily if the floor were covered with thick carpeting? Probably not. The carpeting would rub against the legs of the desk, making it harder to move.

This rubbing is a contact force called **friction.** If you want an object to move quickly, friction can be a problem. If you want to slow a moving object, such as a rowboat, the friction caused by dragging the oars in the water will help.

What happens if more than one force is used on an object? Suppose you and your friend want to use the same towel and are both equally strong. If each of you grabs an end and pulls at the same time using the same amount of force, what do you think will happen? Neither one of you will be able to pull the towel away from the other.

But what would happen if your older brother had helped you? His force, combined with yours, probably would have been greater than your friend's force. Your friend would have lost because the towel would have moved more easily toward the greater force of your brother and you.

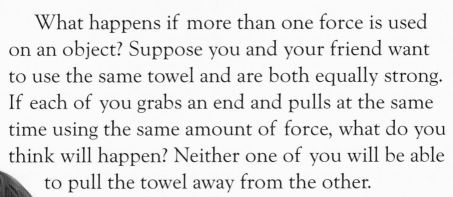

You must use some force to keep your dog from running away while you are walking together.

Force and friction often work together to start and stop motion. Suppose you are going to in-line skate in the park. In order to start skating, you need to push off the ground with one foot. Then you must do the same with the other to keep moving. The more force you use to push off the ground, the faster your speed will be.

What happens if you need to slow down and stop? To do that you need to use friction. If you press your heel down, part of the skate will make contact with the ground and create friction. The friction made by this contact slows your speed. If you continue doing this, you will be able to stop.

There are forces that can move or change an object's position without touching it. These forces are called non-contact forces. **Gravity** is a non-contact force that pulls objects toward each other.

An object's weight is a measurement of how much pull gravity places on it. Your weight is the amount of force with which gravity pulls you toward Earth's center. Weight depends on the mass of an object. An object with more mass will be pulled more strongly by gravity and will weigh more.

You can feel the pull of gravity when you cycle uphill.

Magnet tower

Gravity is not the only non-contact force at work. Have you ever played with magnets? Do you remember how the magnets pulled toward each other as you moved them close together? This pulling is called magnetism. **Magnetism** is a force that pulls on, or attracts, metals that have iron in them. Magnets do not attract objects such as wood or plastic because they do not contain iron.

Did you know that playing is work?

Work

Did you know that you work every time you cause something, including yourself, to move or change position? Scientists think of **work** as the use of force to move an object. Playing tag is actually work, since you are moving your body. The amount of work that is done depends on how much force is used and how far the object is moved.

Think about trying to push a wall again. Even if you pushed as hard as you could and used great force, you would not move that wall. Since work is done only when force makes something move, no work would be done.

Is there another way to move that wall? Maybe you are thinking that a machine could be used to move the wall. You are right to think of using a machine. A machine would be able to push the wall with more force.

Not all machines are big and complicated. Simple machines have few or no moving parts. Inclined planes, wedges, screws, levers, wheels and axles, and pulleys are all simple machines.

How is an inclined plane used? Suppose you need to move a horse into a trailer. A horse is very heavy, so it would be very difficult to carry. But an inclined plane can help.

Ramps are very useful for wheelchair users.

The word *inclined* means "leaning or slanted." A plane is a flat surface. An inclined plane is a ramp. A ramp makes it easier to move an object from a higher position to a lower one, or the reverse.

Walking a horse up a ramp, or

inclined plane, makes it possible to move it into a trailer. The same amount of work, moving the horse, would be done even if an inclined plane were not used. But the inclined plane makes the work a lot easier.

The ramp makes it easier to move the horse into the trailer.

Ramp

Another simple machine that is often used is a wedge. A wedge has one or two slanted sides that end in a sharp edge. You can slide a wedge of wood under a door to hold it in place. You can drive a wedge of metal into a piece of wood to split, or cut, it. The next time your father uses a knife to cut pieces of cake, you can tell him he is using a wedge!

Wedge

This axe is a wedge.

A screw looks very different from an inclined plane or a wedge. It is actually an inclined plane that is wrapped around a center post. This makes ridges. A screw is used to hold things together. Screws are often used to hold furniture together.

If you open a jar, you are using a screw. The inside of the lid has thin ridges around its rim. These ridges form a screw that helps you to raise and lower the jar lid.

A screw

Screw ridges

The lid of this jar is a screw.

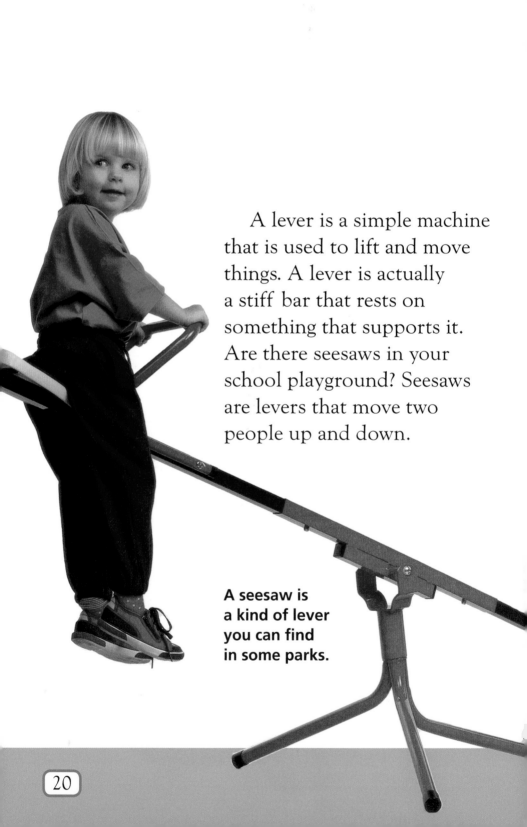

A lever is a simple machine that is used to lift and move things. A lever is actually a stiff bar that rests on something that supports it. Are there seesaws in your school playground? Seesaws are levers that move two people up and down.

A seesaw is a kind of lever you can find in some parks.

Handle

Fishing line

Reel with fishing line

Wheel

Axle

Inside of reel

A wheel and axle is a simple machine. A wheel and axle is used on a fishing rod. The handle of the fishing rod acts as an axle that is attached to the wheel, which contains the fishing line. When the axle, or handle, turns, it causes the wheel to turn. This makes it easier to reel in the fishing line.

Have you ever watched a sailor raise a sail on a sailboat? If so, you have seen a simple machine called a pulley at work. A pulley changes the direction of motion of an object to which a force is applied. This makes it easier to move an object, such as a sail, in a direction that is hard to reach.

A pulley is a grooved wheel and axle over which a rope is pulled. The rope, with the sail tied to it, passes through the pulley. When the sailor pulls down on the rope, the wheel turns and the sail goes up. Now the sail can fill with wind that sends the boat off across the waves.

A pulley is a simple machine.

Pulley wheel

Rope

Load

Things in motion and things at work are all around us. The next time you ride a bike, open a refrigerator, or bounce a ball, think about how much you have learned about motion and work!

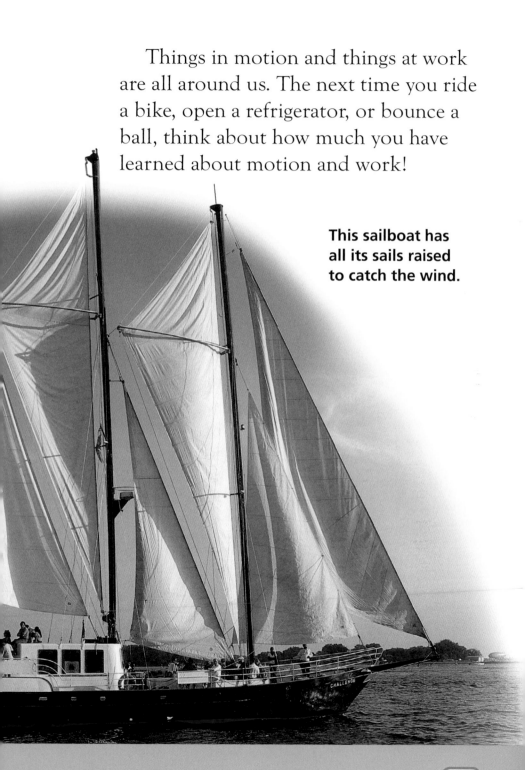

This sailboat has all its sails raised to catch the wind.

Glossary

force a push or pull

friction a contact force that opposes the motion of an object

gravity a non-contact force that pulls objects toward each other

magnetism a non-contact force that attracts metals containing iron

motion a change of position

position the location of an object

relative position the placement of an object compared to another

speed rate at which, or how fast, an object changes its position

work the movement of an object through the use of force